THE BACK HOME SERIES

SERIES TITLES

WRITERS TALKING ABOUT

MICHAEL MARTONE

"This is the name-dropping-est memoir I've ever read, and I told Michael Martone so when I met him at the Essenhaus in Middlebury Township. He was wearing a tan off the rack double breasted suit and had his draft card in the pocket. Martone is one of the few writers who was born in Indiana, writes about Indiana, and eats in Indiana, but meanwhile, he seems to have been everywhere else, too, meeting all the best writers. That's my life, he said. We both ordered the John Barth special, but the Amish maiden brought us mashed potatoes and a tub of fried chicken anyway. 'Tunnel of Fudge Cake for dessert?' I suggested. 'Bluaugh!' said Michael Martone, but he didn't say no."

—BONNIE JO CAMPBELL
National Book Award Finalist
author of *American Salvage* and *The Waters*

"April 1999, I went to Tuscaloosa for an interview at the University of Alabama. After the usual meetings—committee, department chair, dean—Michael Martone walked me to his car and took me on a tour. We talked about our native Midwest as we drove through town. We ended up on a street of brick ranch houses with tidy lawns. 'Faculty live here,' he told me. 'Looks like my parents' neighborhood,' I said. Wordlessly he made a quick U-turn, bumping the curb, and headed downtown. Double-parked in front of a record store called Whirligig, he pointed. 'There are apartments up there.'"

—JOSH RUSSELL
author of *King of the Animals* and *Yellow Jack*

"Was it a conference, a university gig? That's lost, part of that weird era of travel. It was somewhere I didn't live, in a room with students—Martone's, I think, but not Alabama, not Syracuse, so who knows. Martone at the podium, natty in a black suit, pocket square for a pop of color, shock of white hair and owlish glasses. As part of the prefatory remarks, bringing up cellphones—to silence us, we think—he tells a story of receiving a call in the middle of a reading and answering it, folding it into the narrative like a comic pouncing on crowd work. And then, taking the bit further, he holds up his phone, showily turns it off, and then gives us his phone number, encouraging us to text him during the reading, an instruction we receive with glee. He reads, we text. What happened to those extratextual texts? Has Martone woven these into a story he tells as part of his prefatory remarks? Is it a running gag where he cherry picks the very best texts and drops the dross, honing into a polished routine, or does he read and then immediately delete them? Is there a notebook somewhere with the full transcript, an audience that grows with each reading? And what did I text him, sitting in the front row? All lost, except his playful invitation to include us. Are people who came that day to listen still texting him—and does he still have that number? It's possible he's changed carriers and his old number has been assigned to some confused other who now receives this torrent of voices making outre literary puns and curses the number's former owner, this Michael, this Martone, this Michael Martone."

—STEWART O'NAN
author of *Ocean State* and *Henry, Himself*

"*Martone in Syracuse, 1993.* Dark shock of hair, dark-rimmed glasses. The winter is too dark and too long, too lake-effect-snow-freeze-your-freaking-nose-off frigid, and in the ice-crusted streets no one pauses to pass the time. But to your faculty gatherings Martone brings his flat, dry, Midwestern humor. When you gather in restaurants to talk books, poetry, gossip, celebrate famous writers, Martone brings his Fort Wayne-metafiction-autobiographical-half-the-time-you-don't-get-what-he's-talking-about humor, his irony and his wit, his love for his wife and his new-dad-means-everything zeal. Outside, the snow may be falling, and on the streets, among strangers, there may be only that clipped, cold briskness, but Martone is here, he's from Indiana, and he warms you; he makes you laugh. He makes you feel you belong, and you appreciate how he carries that sharp-angled humor so discreetly underneath his Midwestern Nice."

—RILLA ASKEW
American Book Award Winner
author of *The Hungry and the Haunted* and *Fire in Beulah*

"Why am I not in this book? An icy night in Boston, circa 2013, Michael and his wife Theresa and the writer Bryan Furuness and yours and a slippery tumble through the frozen streets of Beantown, chasing down some Thai spot Michael knew about. A glorious campfire of a meal, noodles licking like tiny flames, our warm huddle inside a frigid Boston. Witnesses and witnessing, unknowing agents in the fire, a brilliant recipe for Michael Martone's literary kitchen. Strange anecdotes and stranger laughter. A perfect hootenanny of Martone-ography. Where was your notebook then, Michael? How did you memorialize our tiny, giant evening? How does anyone curate and name mythology? What constitutes history to Michael Martone? Is anything true?"

—ROBERT STAPLETON
editor of *Booth*

TABLE TALK

&

SECOND THOUGHTS

a memoir in flashes

MICHAEL MARTONE

CORNERSTONE PRESS
UNIVERSITY OF WISCONSIN-STEVENS POINT

Cornerstone Press, Stevens Point, Wisconsin 54481
Copyright © 2025 Michael Martone
www.uwsp.edu/cornerstone

Printed in the United States of America by
Point Print and Design Studio, Stevens Point, Wisconsin

Library of Congress Control Number: 2025931781
ISBN: 978-1-960329-77-6

Frontispiece: Plate from "l'Assommoir (man proposing a toast at table with five other people)" by Gaston La Touche, 1878. The Charles Deering Collection. The Art Institute of Chicago.

All interior photographs and illustrations reprinted via public domain.

This is a work of nonfiction. All of the events in this book are true to the best of the author's memory. Some names and identifying features have been changed to protect the identity of certain parties. The author in no way represents any company, corporation, or brand, mentioned herein. The views expressed in this memoir are solely those of the author.

Cornerstone Press titles are produced in courses and internships offered by the Department of English at the University of Wisconsin–Stevens Point.

DIRECTOR & PUBLISHER
Dr. Ross K. Tangedal

EXECUTIVE EDITORS
Jeff Snowbarger, Freesia McKee

EDITORIAL DIRECTOR
Brett Hill

SENIOR EDITOR
Ellie Atkinson

PRESS STAFF
Cora Bender, Kimberly Janesch, Lilly Kulbeck, Sophie McPherson, Madison Schultz, Holly White, Ava Willett, Sam Zajkowski

For John Barth (1930–2024), who set the table.

Pictured, a picture of John Barth teaching in Baltimore.
The table is John Barth's writing table, refinished, in Tuscaloosa.

ALSO BY MICHAEL MARTONE:

FICTION

Alive and Dead in Indiana

Safety Patrol

Fort Wayne Is Seventh on Hitler's List

Pensées: The Thoughts of Dan Quayle

Seeing Eye

The Blue Guide to Indiana

Double-Wide: Collected Fiction of Michael Martone

Four for a Quarter

Winesburg, Indiana: A Fork River Anthology
(with Bryan Furuness)

Memoranda

The Moon over Wapakoneta

*The Complete Writings of Art Smith, the Bird Boy of Fort Wayne,
Edited by Michael Martone*

Plain Air: Sketches from Winesburg, Indiana

The Tiny Book of Forts

NONFICTION

The Flatness and Other Landscapes

Michael Martone

Unconventions: Attempting the Art of Craft and the Craft of Art

Racing in Place: Collages, Fragments, Postcards, Ruins

Brooding: Arias, Choruses, Lullabies, Follies, Dirges, and a Duet

EDITED COLLECTIONS

A Place of Sense: Pieces of the Midwest

Townships: Pieces of the Midwest

Extreme Fiction: Fabulists and Formalists
(with Robin Hemley)

Rules of Thumb

The Scribner Anthology of Contemporary Short Fiction
(with Lex Williford)

Touchstone Anthology of Contemporary Creative Nonfiction
(with Lex Williford)

Not Normal, Illinois: Peculiar Fictions from the Flyover

POETRY

At a Loss

Return to Powers

FEATURING (IN ORDER OF APPEARANCE):

Adrienne Rich
Lance Olsen
Rona Jaffe
Mary Swander
Tim O'Brien
Gish Jen
Theresa Pappas
Mary Gaitskill
George Saunders
Mark Doty
Major Jackson
Darin Strauss
Roxane Gay
C.D. Wright
Michael Cunningham
Susan Neville
John Updike
Kurt Vonnegut
Honoree Fanonne Jeffers
Janet Kauffman
Lillian-Yvonne Bertram
Sue Miller
Doug Bauer
Anne Carson
Hayden Carruth
Joe Geha
Morton Janklow
Jay McInerney
Tama Janowitz
Ken Auletta
Amanda Urban
Gregory Orr
Kevin Young
Dean Young
David St. John
Marge Piercy
Nikki Finney
Janet Desaulnier
Mary Robison
John Barth

John Gardner
Fredrick Barthelme
Moira Crone
Liz Rosenberg
Molly Peacock
Andrei Codrescu
Louise Glück
Richard Rhodes
Mark Kramer
Fenton Johnson
Nick Flynn
William H. Gass
Rikki Ducornet
Denis Johnson
Carol Bly
Noah Bly
Gay Talese
Czesław Miłosz
Gerald Stern
Jorie Graham
Valerie Miner
Linda Gregerson
James A. Michener
Michael Wilkerson
Lorrie Moore
Anthony Doerr
Madison Smartt Bell
Cris Mazza
Lucie Brock-Brodio
Jonathan Lethem
Andy Duncan
Sydney Duncan
Jodi Picoult
Tomaz Salamun
Lois Metzger
Stephen Dunn
Tom Lux
Mary Ruefle
Edmund White
Richard Howard

John Irwin
Stephen Dixon
Jane Smiley
Patricia Henley
Allen Grossman
Hugh Kenner
Ross Gay
Don Belton
W.D. Snodgrass
Robert Novak
Charles Baxter
Heather McHugh
Mas'ud Zavarzadeh
Ellen Bryant Voight
Lewis Hyde
John Kenneth Galbraith
Arthur Schlesinger
B. F. Skinner
Melanie Rae Thon
Robert Day
E.O. Wilson
Mark Strand
Jonathan Franzen
David Foster Wallace
Raymond Carver
Tess Gallagher
Kenneth Rosen
Andre Dubus
Robley Wilson, Jr.
Christopher Leland
Pam Houston
William Stafford
Safiya Henderson-Holmes
George Starbuck
Jay Brandon
Donald Barthelme
Adam Cohen
Amy Hempel
Juan Reyes
Junot Diaz
Michael Rosen
Lidia Yuknavitch

Doug Hesse
Becky Bradway
Robert Stone
Robin Hemley
Rosanna Warren
Elizabeth Spires
Louise Erdrich
Seamus Heaney
Joyce Carol Oates
Rick Moody
Laurel Nakadate
Neil Nakadate
Andrea Barrett
Debra Spark
Judith Grossman
Brian Evenson
Grace Paley
Wendell Berry
Maury Telleen
Bill Knott
Marie Howe
Mary Karr
Richard Russo
C.J. Hribal
ZZ Packer
T. C. Boyle
Robert Olen Butler
Joyce Johnson
Lydia Davis
Franz Wright
Francine Prose
Roxana Robinson
Jane Owen
David Shields
Maya Sonenberg
Jim Harrison
Brad Watson
George Plimpton
Barry Hannah
Richard Yates
Samuel Delany
Neil Gaiman

. . . poetry makes nothing happen . . .

—W.H. Auden, "In Memory of W.B. Yeats"

Trains

Tuscaloosa, 2010

Adrienne Rich and I ended up talking about trains at dinner after her reading. She asked about the train trestle she'd seen crossing the Black Warrior River. I told her that the L&N, the GM&O, and the Southern all had depots here. We talked about conductors and their watches and how time had been reinvented by the railroads. Not poetry, but not not poetry. Train jargon, for those who know it, is a kind of poetry. "I'll call you Train Man," she said and did the rest of the evening, and she left town knowing me as no one other.

Big Love

Salt Lake City, 2010

The scale of Salt Lake City was difficult to judge. The mountains seemed to emerge in the middle of the city. At night, looking down to the city's distorted but tidy grid of lights from Lance Olsen's apartment, I thought of those simulations demonstrating how space warped, a vast quilt wrinkled by an invisible rolling gravity. I asked Lance about the hotel the university had booked for me and how the room where I was staying was so out of proportion. The bed seemed to be, at least, double king-sized. The sink in the bathroom came up to my chest. The ceiling was not like a cathedral but cathedral. Lance explained I had gotten one of the rooms for visiting NBA players. He agreed with me when I said Salt Lake City was Borgesian, a map more detailed than the thing it represents. Later, that night, lost in the giant bed beneath its oversized quilt, I watched an episode of Big Love on a screen that easily took up one whole wall of an infinite room.

Best

Cambridge, 1987

Rona Jaffe hosted a lunch at Radcliffe for the judges of the creative writing award she had endowed. This was the first year of the prize, and she was excited about promoting the contest and aiding aspiring women writers. I was the only man at the table. Harvard had a very small creative writing program. There were four or five other judges drawn from other departments. She told us stories about her time at Radcliffe, moving to New York to work in publishing, and then writing a novel about a Radcliffe woman moving to New York and working in publishing, *The Best of Everything*. It was made into a movie. She had known Joan Crawford. Radcliffe, then, was still home to its publishing course. As a group, we talked about what we might expect to see, subjects and styles, in the many submissions we knew the contest would generate. As I left, I mentioned to her that it appeared graduates now were not moving to the City but right to LA, writing for the movies and TV. "The men and the women?" she asked. Yes, I assured her, both.

Clothesline

Ames, 1984

Mary Swander lived north of downtown, up Duff, near the hospital. She had just moved to town, hired by Iowa State, but was from Iowa. She was one of a few writers from Iowa who lived in Iowa and wrote about Iowa. In the post office downtown, the mural over the postmaster's door pictured *The History of Corn*. The post office itself reeked, steeped by all the perfume and cologne sample cards advertisers inserted in magazines and catalogues. The odors expanded, tainting all the mail, lingering in the lobby, escaping from the sorting room in the back. Mary had environmental and chemical sensitivities, bad allergic reactions to such smells. Her response was so severe that in her syllabi she asked her students to refrain from using scented soaps and shampoos. Driving up Duff in the spring after a long winter, I saw Mary hanging her mail on the backyard clothesline to air out. I told her that my grandmother always said I should get out more, "Blow the stink off of you!"

Draft

Denver, 2000

I showed Tim O'Brien my draft card in Bin Ramke's living room. I was designated 1H. That meant 1 Holding. My lottery number when I graduated high school had been 48, but the last induction had been the year before. I told him my grandfather had worked at a filling station, Standard Oil, across the street from the Selective Service Office in Fort Wayne. The draftees, waiting for the bus to take them to Indianapolis for their physicals, huddled in the station to keep warm, buy pop and candy, and use the payphone that made a pinging sound when you fed in the coins. It was still a full-service filling station, and the cars pulling in the driveway would run over wired hoses that triggered a flat bell in the garage. We always used to say that the Midwest was so flat that nothing stopped the wind racing down from the mountains out west. Tim, who grew up in Minnesota, said, "We used to say that too," where he came from.

Gasp

Cambridge, 1989

Now when I give a reading, I think of Gish Jen. I always make sure to check the order of pages I am reading from. Are they in the right order? I was reading a long story in the Dolphin Moon Series at the Cambridge Y in Central Square. I was new in town and many local writers had come out to hear me. I wanted to make a good impression. Theresa was there with Sam, who was just a baby, asleep when I started to read. The story was building nicely to an exciting ending. All the pages were in order. As I finished reading the last full page, I realized I had run out of pages. The ending page was missing. The pages had all been in order but not all there. I had to stop and confess to the audience what had happened. Theresa, in the back of the room, gasped and woke up the baby with a start. Gish Jen, sitting next to them, gasped too as I paraphrased the ending. I now check that the pages are in order and all there.

Leather

Tuscaloosa, 2003

It was March in Tuscaloosa, warm already, but Mary Gaitskill and George Saunders arrived from Syracuse wearing leather jackets. It was still winter up north. Their visit was being funded out of the Bankhead Endowment. The Bankheads are a prominent Alabama family. Tallulah's family. Mary liked that she was getting Bankhead money. They did separate workshops that morning at the student center, a joint reading that night. After the classes, heading to lunch, Mary realized her leather jacket had disappeared, and wasn't where she left it when she went in to teach. I spent the afternoon tracking it down. The building wasn't a classroom building. It housed offices, the student bookstore, the cafeteria, boardrooms, ballrooms. There were many lost-and-founds. The reading that night went off without a hitch, though both Mary and George still seemed to be ducks out of water. That's often the case when writers visit. Alabama is its own thing. Putting on his leather jacket after the reception, George said to me that they'd have to have me come back up to Syracuse one day soon. That never worked out.

Nerf

Chicago, 2012

The Literary Death Match was held at Buddy Guy's bar, and Mark Doty and I (somehow) were judges. I first met Mark twenty years before in Iowa when he was teaching at Drake and writing poems with Ruth as MR Doty. We remembered together in between making calls, shooting the losers (Major Jackson, Darin Strauss, and Roxane Gay—even though she turned out to be the winner) with spongy darts launched from Nerf guns. It was late by the time we made it out to the street to say goodnight. "We've come a long way from Iowa." The streets of Chicago were filled with drunken poets and writers in town for the AWP convention.

Quonset Hut

Kalamazoo, 2000

Six years before she would die suddenly (thrombosis, a blood clot), C.D. Wright and I were readers at the Third Coast Writers Conference. Between events, I asked her about "The South" (I was new to living in "The South"), where she was from, and Rhode Island, where she lived now. I asked her if she had ever seen Cutty Hunk, the last island in the Elizabeth chain, or been to Quonset Point. *Quonset,* I told her, was one of my favorite words. Place names! We had to talk about "Kalamazoo," where we found ourselves, now, talking about place names. It was a song before it knew it was a song, she said. All those A's and O's.

Slush

Tuscaloosa, 2004

I remember asking Michael Cunningham if he remembered reading a story of mine he found in the *Iowa Review*'s slush pile years ago. It was a story about Alfred Kinsey and Indiana, and it was published in the *Iowa Review* in 1979. When I saw the editor of the journal at a conference years later, he told me that Michael Cunningham, who had been a graduate student assistant back then, found the story in the slush pile. Then, years later, walking with Michael to Smith Hall, where he would read from his novel *The Hours*, I asked if he remembered finding my story in the slush pile all those years ago. He said he did, and he remembered passing it on to the editor who would publish it. "There were so many stories," I remember him saying, "and yours just stood out." "Yes," I remember saying, "so many stories."

Toothbrush

Indianapolis, 1996

Susan Neville remembers it differently. She remembered John Updike, sitting behind her as she drove the minivan, pointing out that there was a toothbrush on the dashboard. I don't remember the toothbrush at all. I was sitting shotgun in the minivan with Kurt Vonnegut behind me. In the shadows, I couldn't see Vonnegut even though my head was turned to listen to him talk to Updike. I could see Updike in the pale light and a smear of the melting limestone wedding cake of a building, Jordan Hall, in the window behind him as we drove through the campus to the venue where they would speak keynotes at the inaugural Place and Spirit Festival. That is what I remember, not the toothbrush but Vonnegut pointing out Jordan Hall and saying something about limestone, Indiana architecture, and his father's buildings— the telephone exchanges and the drug stores. I remember, too, Susan's slight smile, lit by the van's dashboard lights, as she listened, negotiating the narrow street that led over to the sheer floodlit limestone cliffs of Clowes Hall in the near distance.

Yachts

Tuscaloosa, 2000

I had driven Honoree Fanonne Jeffers to North River Yacht Club where she would give a reading from her new book *The Gospel of Barbecue*. She had graduated from Alabama a few years before I arrived to teach. We sat in the car in the parking lot of the Yacht Club, the tony country club overlooking an artificial lake. The paper company had built it on paper company land in the 70s when it became more profitable to grow houses and golf courses than pine trees. Jack Warner, who owned the paper company, also owned the largest collection of American Colonial Art in the country. The Smithsonian asked him every year if he would will the art to them, I told Honoree. We talked about local barbecue. Tuscaloosa is located at the intersection of red and yellow sauces. And we were (are?) both Hoosiers. She was born in Kokomo. What did it mean to be a writer of "place" when writing in some other place? Inside, the Yacht Club's walls were filled with 18th century American art, so many folk-art renderings of Washingtons on white horses.

Tiles

Hudson, 1999

One thing I remember about my trip was the famous water tower located on the highest point in Ypsilanti. Janet Kauffman drove us by it on the way to her house in the country. I grew up not too far away in Indiana. It's a glacial plain and had been swampy hardwood bog until it was cleared and drained. Janet's place had been a farm, a farm surrounded by farms, farms in fencerow-to-fencerow corn and beans now. Her place had been a farm, but now she was letting it go wild. She was letting the place be what it wanted to be. She wanted me to see how it was coming back, show me how she had broken the tiles, the tiles buried underground. There were pools now and ponds percolating. The ground where we walked was spongy. Bramble and scrub sprouted from seeds that had been dormant for one hundred years. Same thing happened when they broke the tiles in the Limberlost in Indiana too. It was wild and beautiful. Her neighbors thought she'd gone mad, she said, and patrolled their properties' borders looking to staunch the leakage.

Seltzer

Montpelier, 2008

While Lillian-Yvonne Bertram took my picture, we tried to remember all the flavors of Polar Seltzer, including the limited editions. Raspberry Lime, Orange Vanilla, Strawberry Watermelon, Blueberry Lemonade, Georgia Peach, Mandarin, Triple Berry, Black Cherry, Pomegranate, Cranberry Lime. Polar wasn't distributed then in Alabama, where I lived. Since then, for several years, Lillian-Yvonne would send me postcards naming the new flavors as they came out. Toasted Coconut, Ruby Red Grapefruit, Cranberry Clementine. In the pictures they took (I used them as author photos for a few years), my hair is still long, escaping out from under my old Tuscan vintner's hat. I am wearing old sunglasses, and it looks like I am looking into the sun.

Pudding

Cambridge, 1985

It was our first dinner party since moving to Cambridge from Iowa. Sue Miller and Doug Bauer's house. Doug was from Iowa. Sue's novel, *The Good Mother*, was coming out, and they had just returned from Paris. Everyone said what their favorite arrondissement was. For dessert, there was a chocolate mousse. "What a great chocolate mousse," someone said. Sue thanked them but said, "no, not a mousse, a pudding."

Neptune or Poseidon

Asheville, unknown

I can't find any record that Anne Carson was there. In Swannanoa, North Carolina, teaching with me at Warren Wilson College one residency. Nothing. I think I remember her wearing webbed gloves on her way to swim laps. We ate dinner once together at a seafood place near the Waffle House out on the highway leading into Asheville. It was named The Neptune or The Poseidon. I don't remember. I don't remember what we ordered. Fish. Fish, I'd guess. But what kind? I do remember her questioning if it was a good idea to order ocean fish up in the mountains this far from any ocean.

Keeping

Syracuse, 1993

Hayden Carruth had retired the year before I arrived in Syracuse after teaching at the university for a dozen years. He lived out in the country, in Munnsville, but would come into the city on weekends for dinner parties and readings. Once, we all watched a video of the new movie, *Brother's Keeper,* about the four Ward Brothers: the death of one of them and the murder trial of another. Hayden knew them. They were his neighbors. He was able to provide commentary as the bleak documentary played. We all watched the dark, deeply shadowed pictures of the illiterate and inarticulate brothers punctuated by Hayden's understated poetic footnotes. In the end, nothing was resolved. Was it murder, or was it death by natural causes? There was not enough evidence either way, and as with all stories, there were many points-of-view and several different ways to narrate what transpired or remember what exactly had happened.

Gamey

Story City, 1981

"The kids need new shoes," Joe Geha said as he drove me up to Story City. The VFW was having their "Wild Game Night." It was a "Stag" and an "All You Can Eat" of deer, boar, squirrel, dove, pigeon, possum, duck, goose, pheasant, and quail. Bear and bison. There was barnyard rooster. Goat. Llama and guinea pig. Games of Chance were set up all around the room, illegal, but this was a fundraiser for the Post. Deputies in uniform were playing craps. County farmers and hands played all kinds of card games, spooning down stews and burgoos from pressed paper bowls beside them. Everyone smoked cigars and cigarettes, retelling the hunting stories about the meat we were eating. Everything was greasy. The rooster did not taste like chicken. Joe played poker and told stories about Toledo (Ohio, not Iowa), distracting the other players. He won enough money, he said, for a shoe and a half for his two kids, Megan and Katie. The big Story City sign, an arrow pointing into town, was dark when we drove by it on our way back to Ames.

Double-Breasted

New York, 1993

I was told I had to look presentable, so I went to J. C. Penney and bought a tan, off-the-rack suit, double-breasted. It was Morton Janklow's party, but it was really a party Syracuse was giving for Morton Janklow, an alumnus. The next day the Chancellor would take him to lunch at the Four Seasons and make the ask, a million dollars. He ended up giving the money to Columbia. Everyone was there at the Lubin House. I was drinking cranberry juice. In my new suit, I joked that I was some kind of Dapper Don with the bartender. I asked if he was an aspiring actor moonlighting. No, he said, I want to be what they are. He pointed to Jay McInerney, Tama Janowitz, Ken Auletta, and Amanda Urban, talking in a group on the other side of the room. I'm a writer, he said, like them. At the dinner that night, the frosting of the chocolate cake was sprinkled with flecks of edible gold.

Close Shave

Swannanoa, 1989

At the residency, everyone stayed in an old dorm and used communal bathrooms. Once I was shaving at a sink next to Gregory Orr, who was shaving at another sink next to me. We looked at each other shaving in the mirrors over the sinks. I mentioned to him that his book, *Gathering the Bones Together*, was one of my favorite books of poems. He nodded, and we kept on shaving. The book had drawings by Brad Holland, surreal pen and ink drawings, and I remember thinking how our heads in the mirrors looked as if they could be another drawing from the book. Our faces lathered and his impressive mustache emerging through the foam.

Church

Tuscaloosa, 2004

Kevin Young and I were talking about moving and how each place comes with its own unique question you get asked when you arrive some new place usually by the realtor showing you around. He was living in Atlanta at the time and had come over to Tuscaloosa to give a reading. Before that, he had lived in Indiana, and we agreed that "What work do you do?" was an Indiana and Rust Belt initial question. "Virginia's," I said, "would be, 'Who are your people?'" The longtime editor of the *Iowa Review* always said Iowa's was "What will you garden?" "The South?" I asked. Kevin didn't hesitate. It was a statement more than a question. "What church will you go to?"

Dinged

Bloomington, 1976

Dean Young and I were in the same undergraduate poetry workshop at Indiana. We always argued about line breaks. He had his reasons, and I had mine. I got so mad. I went home and wrote a new poem. I ended the line when the typewriter's bell dinged. When the bell dinged, I ended the line even when the bell dinged in the middle of a word. Why, Dean asked after he read the new poem, did you end the line there? I said I ended the line there because the fucking bell dinged. And ever since then, my poetry has always looked like prose with a justified left margin and a very ragged right one.

Galaxy

Bethany Beach, 1980

On the way to Bethany Beach in Delaware, the highway went near the Dover Air Force Base. A C-5 Galaxy, a huge cargo plane, was taking off, so big it was a lumbering gray cloud that seemed not to fly so much as to float, inching up off the ground. At the beach, David St. John had rented a converted old church. The big echoing nave still had the pews arranged in rows. David was drinking tequila shots up where the altar once had been. The salt. The shot. The lime wedge. The drinks seemed to have no effect on him. Much later, we wandered out to the backyard, looked up at the night sky. It was very dark. No yard lights. A few streetlights. We could hear the ocean and see the giant shadows of the cargo planes descending, blotting out the stars.

Kale

Ames, 1983

Purple kale, a leaf or two, was used as a garnish at the fancy restaurants, a step up from simple sprigs of parsley. Kale looked particularly good on a plate of pasta like fettuccine Alfredo, which was also exotic back then too. We took Marge Piercy to Lucullan's before her reading, a new restaurant in town. A TV over the bar was tuned to MTV. Madonna was dancing. "Do you want your kale? It's edible," she said. Each white plate wiped clean with the white bread had a leaf or two left over. We offered them all to her. She ate the kale readily.

Naan

Dayton, 2001

Nikky Finney and I, along with a dozen other writers, taught one summer for the Ohio State Arts Council at Wright State University outside Dayton. For one dinner a group of us went searching for this Indian restaurant out beyond the AFB and Museum. We found it finally. It was a family-run place and pretty much empty but for the family gathered around a big TV, watching a Bollywood musical that they turned off when we sat down. After we ordered, Nikky insisted that they turn the movie back on, and they did. We shared all the dishes, and there was lots of naan, and planes flew overhead, landing at the nearby airfields. There were leftovers, too, that we took home. Our hotel rooms had little fridges and microwaves.

Published

Iowa City, 1981

I was working, having just started to teach at Iowa State University in Ames. I would drive over to Iowa City on the weekends to visit several of my friends, who were now in the Writers Workshop, poets with MAs now getting MFAs. They took me to their hangout bar, Dave's Fox Head. The bar was crowded with poets and writers. I was at the bar ordering drinks for the table. A woman next to me introduced herself to me. "Hello!" she said, "My name is Janet Desaulnier, and I just had a story taken by *The New Yorker*." Before I could respond, I immediately thought that such an icebreaking line would only work at a bar in Iowa City. I congratulated her and told her I was teaching in Ames and had driven over to visit my friends who were poets and writers too. Just then, one of my friends came up to the bar to help me carry the drinks back to the table.

Seeds

Baltimore, 1977 & 1982

I wasn't there, but only heard about it from Mary Robison who was there. She told me later. A bunch of us were having brunch at John Barth's house a day after an alumni reading at Johns Hopkins. John Gardner's visit to Jack's classroom. Gardner was being treated at the Hopkins Hospital, and Jack invited him, expecting, she thought, a lively chat between friends, literary colleagues. Instead, John turned to Jack, right there in front of the students, and said something about wasting our lives, writing self-conscious, meta-fictional, alienating prose. "Instead, we should be doing Dickensian Transparent Realism." Later, Jack would call what happened "Literary Kneecapping." There that day, besides Mary, were Fredrick Barthelme, Moira Crone, Liz Rosenberg, and Molly Peacock. Mary, when she told me about it later, thought that it seemed to her to be a deathbed conversion. She thought he thought he was dying and regretted writing *Grendel*, a book about a book. "We should," she told me, "tap into the emotion of our own personal messy stories," as we finished up the everything bagels, the seeds getting everywhere.

The War

Baltimore, 1980

Andrei Codrescu stood out in Baltimore, stood apart. He told us: "Thirty-third and Greenmount, a place of great power!" One day, he appeared in an olive drab army jacket. It had many pockets. Sonny's Surplus was on Greenmount. "Nice jacket, Andrei," we said. "Thank you very much," he said. "Where did you get the jacket?" we asked. "In the war," he said. "The war!" we said. "Andrei, what war?" "The War of the Jackets," he said.

X-Acto

Syracuse, 1993

During the small talk at dinner that night, I wanted to ask Louise Glück about the X-Acto knife. Her father, I thought, had invented it for use as a scalpel, but it couldn't be cleaned. We had been talking about the white space between the print in a collage. I mentioned Francis Ponge and how she was interested in everyday objects like soap and knives. Louise cut in right there: "She," she said, "wasn't a *she* but a *he*." Right then, dessert arrived.

Wursthaus

Cambridge, 1986

We were eating lunch, Richard Rhodes and I, at the Wursthaus in Harvard Square. I had just moved to Cambridge to teach at Harvard. He had blurbed my book, *Alive and Dead in Indiana*. I had been introduced to him by Mark Kramer when I was in Iowa teaching a course called Contemporary Rural and Agricultural Literature. And we talked in the Wursthaus, years later, about an essay in his book *Inland Ground* that I taught, "Watching the Animals," and the slaughterhouse he visited and the home for boys where he grew up and where he helped slaughter cattle and pigs. We were eating sauerbraten and schnitzel. I told him about the move from Iowa to Massachusetts, how strange it had been. And I asked him if he knew what a "Battle Tux" was. He did. I had just learned about them the other day. He seemed to know everything about everything. The book *The Making of the Atomic Bomb* was about to come out.

Suite

Salt Lake City, 2003

That summer, Writers @ Work put us up in a dorm at Westminster College. I shared a suite with Fenton Johnson and Nick Flynn. The building was nice and new. We each had a little bedroom and bath and shared a kitchenette and sitting room with a television and radio. It was nothing like the cramped little dorm rooms I lived in as an undergraduate. A bed, a desk. Shared showers down the hall. Huge dining hall on the ground floor. A common room where the floor watched one TV. Fenton and Nick had read from their memoirs. Workshops of nonfiction writing were overenrolled, lasted all day. We would head back to the dorm, worn out, and rest a bit before going out to dinner. We had breakfast and lunch in the suite's kitchenette. That day we hurried back to the suite, turned on NPR to hear if the decision had come down in *Lawrence v. Texas*. It had. We listened for the details, turned on the TV, but there was no more new news there. That was all anyone talked about that night at dinner in downtown Salt Lake City.

Sections

Cambridge, 1990

I was asked to introduce William H. Gass when he gave the Tanner Lecture at Harvard. When I first read "In the Heart of the Heart of the Country" a dozen years before in an undergraduate class, I thought two things:

> *How did he get me to read a 36 page "story" where nothing happens?*

> *You can write about Indiana?*

I mentioned in my introduction that I drove around Indiana looking for all the towns that began with the letter "B." When a story doesn't have a beginning, middle, and end like that story, usually there is a different kind of organization. That story has 36 titled sections. Later, I excitedly told him my theory about the 36 sections, not 35, not 37. Because, I said, there are 36 sections in a township grid, the township sections that checkerboard the flat landscape of the Midwest. He looked at me and didn't say yes. But he didn't say no either.

Mountains

Denver, 1999

I have never seen the mountains when I have been in Denver. I've been taken out to look at the range, but all I ever see is a big bank of clouds off in the distance. The only time I have ever lost my voice was in Denver. Perhaps it was the altitude . . . I was to give a reading at the University of Denver. I couldn't speak. Squeaks and ragged whispers. Rikki Ducornet, who had taken me out to show me the mountains I never ended up seeing, gave me tea tree oil. I had never seen or heard of tea tree oil. I didn't know what to do with it, and, without a voice, I couldn't speak to ask. I ended up gargling with it. But that didn't help. Rikki read aloud what I was going to read while I sat silently next to her.

Jesus

Syracuse, 1995

There would be one last big snowstorm that spring, on April Fools' Day. It wouldn't close the university, of course. This was Central New York, in lake-effect's shadow, in the unbuckled Snowbelt. It was also the Burned-Over District where the revivals of The Second Great Awakening began. I hadn't gone to the party after Denis Johnson's reading. At the reading, the stories from *Jesus' Son* thrummed, even gaining power as they were read and reread now a few years after they were published. My son, Nick, had just been born, so I walked home after the reading, down Euclid, propelled by the words, to tell Theresa about the reading and the way he read, cool, almost shyly. I wasn't much of a partier then, even less a partier now. The next day, walking up Euclid, I knew what was about to happen. I had gotten a call that morning, waking me. A graduate student, a young woman, would file a grievance. Something had happened at the party. I didn't know what then. It had nothing to do with Denis, but he had been there. And the graduate student would have a story to tell.

Gag

Syracuse, 1991

One never knows what one will get when listening to Carol Bly read one of her stories. She wrote, revised, and finished the story by presenting succeeding drafts in subsequent readings. She started with a few notes, improvised on the spot, playing off the audience's reaction. She taped the "readings" and, after each, transcribed what she had spoken. She used the transcription as the script for the next reading, adding things or deleting, as the new audience responded. Attending the initial reading, one would be struck by the slightness, the sketchiness. In the later readings, the story—its presentation, timing, and detail—had been worked out through many iterations. Noah Bly, Carol's son, had been my student before I came to Syracuse and revealed his mother's method. Carol did a workshop at Syracuse, insisting that there be no "gag rule." The writer under consideration was not to remain silent during the critique. She found it sadistic, she said. Stories were meant, for her, to have a point, to be as relentlessly argumentative as an essay. That night at the reading, we were amazed. Carol "read" to us a whole story from memory.

Developing

Tuscaloosa, 2010

The office that "develops" donors to the university always assigns the prospect to a specific department or program. In this way, not everyone is making an "ask" to the same famous alum for money. Harper Lee, for example, might have been assigned to creative writing, but she was so important the president of the university was the only one able to approach her. Gay Talese was a graduate of the journalism school at Alabama, so the College of Communication was developing him. But they would call me when Mr. Talese visited because I was the only other "creative" writer they knew who wore a hat, coat, and tie. I was Italian too. The two of us walked around campus, time travelers in our get-ups, noting the things that had changed since he had been a student. I bought him lunch at SWEN where we didn't talk about writing much. We talked about Chinese food in New York, where in Italy our families hailed from, and his father's haberdashery in New Jersey. I couldn't and didn't make an "ask," but we talked about how curious the "ask" is and what goes into the asking.

Cake

I–35, Iowa, 1983

I owa State University lent me a car (I didn't have a car) to go to the Des Moines airport to pick up Czesław Miłosz and drive him back to Ames for a lecture and a reading. A Polish math professor went with me. On the trip there, we talked about the work in the fields. Miłosz had just won the Nobel Prize, and on the way back, I pointed out the harvested and turned fields on both sides of the highway. The dirt looks like chocolate cake, he said. The math professor in the back seat said then that they were going to speak in Polish now, and they did all the rest of the way back to Ames. I understood nothing.

Bagel

Iowa City, 1996

The instructors teaching at the Iowa Summer Writing Festival stayed in the Iowa House Hotel in the Iowa Memorial Union. There was a dining room on the ground floor with big windows that overlooked a patio next to the Iowa River. Gerald Stern, one morning, asked me to join him for breakfast there. He was finishing up. I had a plain bagel on my tray, cream cheese in plastic tubs that I would spread on the untoasted bagel with a plastic knife. He had taught at the Writers Workshop for many years and now was retired, but he came back for the Summer Festival. After breakfast and before classes started that day, I wanted to see the new Frank Gehry building next door. He looked at his bagel and said, "An Iowa bagel is an Iowa bagel."

Babies

Port Townsend, 1989

We were riding with Jorie Graham in a van on the way from Sea-Tac to Port Townsend and Fort Warden. We had the baby with us, eight months old. We lived in Medford then. I taught at Harvard and Theresa taught at Tufts. Jorie was in Iowa. Jim Gavin and their daughter, Emily, were in the van too. "Helen Vendler loves kids!" Jorie yelled over the van's noise. "She would love to babysit!" We slept in an old army barrack at night. It was summer. The big old windows were open. Sam cried at night, and that is how we met Valerie Miner, who was trying to sleep on the floor above us.

Bundt

Swannanoa, 2005

Outside it was snowing heavily. The wet snow caught on the pine tree branches and the rhododendron leaves. I had breakfast that day in the kitchen of the dorm where all the Warren Wilson faculty stayed. I didn't want to go to the cafeteria because of the snow. I was eating a bagel and reading the obituaries of *The New York Times* to Linda Gregerson, who was making her breakfast. That morning, the morning it snowed, I read that H. David Dalquist had died. He was 86. He founded Nordic Ware and invented the modern Bundt pan in 1950. He trademarked the name, used modern materials to make it, and added the signature regular folds, a guide for cutting slices. The invention really took off, the obit said, when a recipe for a Tunnel of Fudge Cake took second prize in the 1966 Pillsbury Bake-Off. Linda listened raptly, and then she wanted to read the obit aloud, glossing the story as she read. I listened, chewing my bagel. We both thought then that there had to be, had to be, a poem in there someplace.

Decoy

Baltimore, 1980

James A. Michener had finished his newest novel, *Ches-apeake*, an epic historical fiction narrative of the region. He lived in St. Michaels on the Eastern Shore, researching and writing the novel. I never met him, I missed the reading he gave when he was invited to Johns Hopkins to lecture. I had been positive the other student writers would attend. I was distracted, trying to finish the little book of stories that would become my thesis. My stories were set in Indiana, but I didn't want them to be about the expected Hoosier sub-jects—basketball, cornfields, and the 500. I thought I would avoid what I thought *Chesapeake* would be about—blue crabs, geese, sailboats, and duck decoys. The other student writers didn't attend either. I think we all thought that the *literary* was more important than the *commercial*. Our professors let us know of their disappointment. I was embarrassed that I blew off the chance to meet Michener. Soon after, he moved west to Texas and settled in Austin where he wrote *Space, Texas,* and *Mexico*.

Flamingoes

Madison, 1984

As undergraduates, Michael Wilkerson and I wrote poems on the streets of Bloomington on any subject. We called ourselves RKO Radio Poets and charged twenty-five cents, our motto being "A Poem Must Not Mean But Be Twenty-Five Cents." Now Michael was teaching at the University of Wisconsin in Madison, and he invited me there when my first book came out. Lorrie Moore had just joined the faculty. We told her about Leon Varjian, who had traveled from Indiana to Wisconsin too, and famously constructed the submerged Statue of Liberty on a frozen Lake Mendota and, in the spring, filled the Hill with a huge flock of pink plastic flamingoes. It was all new to Lorrie. We found it all difficult to believe, hard to take seriously where we now found ourselves, lost in staid ancient institutions that seemed to tolerate, for now, our silly juxtapositions. The reading took place in Helen C. White Hall, a concrete Brutalist building constructed in response to the unrest of the 1960s. It was designed to be difficult, almost impossible, to find a doorway in. It took a while, but I did.

Hello

Warren Wilson College, 2008

The first iPhone I saw was Anthony Doerr's. At dusk, a group of us were gathered around him, outside of the dorm where we were staying, waiting on the van that would take us into Asheville for dinner. He held up the black plastic puck, searching for a signal. Its flat screen flickered. Fireflies flickered in the rhododendrons all around us as if they were talking to each other. Earlier that day, Tony had given a lecture on "defamiliarization" and how we get used to the strangeness of the world. The funny thing is, he said, I don't even use it as a phone, and showed us how the letters of the keyboard that popped up exploded when he touched the twitching glass-like panel cupped in the palm of his hand.

More Mountains

Stonington, 1990

I ran into Madison Smartt Bell on Main Street in Stonington's small downtown. Sam, who was small then and could
still ride in the backpack, wanted to get down and throw
rocks into the water. Sam pointed out to the thoroughfare,
where the schooners, at anchor overnight, were now hauling
up their sails. One of them had black sails. One red. But
most were white or off-white. We had all come to Deer Isle
to write something new that summer, thinking it would be
quiet. A mistake. Stonington was still a working harbor. The
pick-up trucks, stacked with lobster traps, ground down the
hill next to the house we rented, waking us before dawn.
Madison was staying on the other side of town. He had
begun work on books about Haiti. That was the first time I
heard the proverb: Dèyè mòn, gen mòn. Sam, too close to
the water, looked for more stones to throw. Madison and I
looked out at the schooners, their paying passengers hauling
at the halyards, set sails looking like mountain ranges. We
told each other what we would write that summer.

Pregnant Midge

Tuscaloosa, 2000

I had cleared out a couple of shelves in my office for Cris Mazza to use. She was the Coal Royalty Writer-in-Residence that fall. Besides books, I kept a collection of toys in the bookcases. Fantastic Four action figures. Crash Test Dummies. Models of the real red tractors I drove on farms in Iowa. I kept Syracuse China dishes and coffee cups, seconds, I got when I taught there. And I had a *Pregnant Midge, Barbie's Friend*™ mint in the box. Walmart no longer sold them after customers complained. "Alabama," I said to Cris. She gave me a trucker's baseball cap advertising Cooper Tires. I told her that most people think the endowment for her position was given by the Coal family. That wasn't the case. The truth was that the university owned land that produced natural gas, methane, and she was being paid out of the royalties generated. I offered to show her the fields if she wanted. That was the year a colleague who got HBO taped *The Sopranos*, and the VHS cassette was shared, passed around the department so no one would get behind on the story.

Scrod

Cambridge, 1985

I had known Lucie Brock-Brodio since graduate school in Baltimore. Now, in Cambridge, she asked me for tips on how to get hired at Harvard. I told her that the lunch at the faculty club would be a big deal and to order scrod. My friend, another poet, Nancy Esposito, told me to order scrod, and I had, and I got the job. Lucie said, "But I never eat in public." It was true. I had never seen her eat. I told her I thought ordering scrod would be enough. "Just move it around on the plate while you are talking." She did. And she did get the job.

Sub-Hunting

Brunswick, 2001

In Maine, we played Mafia. Jonathan Lethem led us in this new party game he knew. There were teams of Insiders and Outsiders. There was "The Mafia." There were "The Innocents." There were sustained periods of discussions filled with shared secrets and deliberate deceptions. The teams were made up of other writers and participants of the Stonecoast Writers Conference. We played after the workshops and readings each evening. People were eliminated, whacked. They slept with the fishes, which seemed right as we were in Maine. The survivors went on playing into the night. I met Jonathan the year before in Tuscaloosa when he visited his friends, the writers Andy and Sydney Duncan. We had played Mafia then too. In Maine, after I was murdered, I went outside and watched the slowly descending sub-hunting P-3 Orion airplanes, home from a mission over the Atlantic, circle over the pine trees, then approach for a landing at the Naval Air Station over in Brunswick.

Vox Balaenae

Cambridge, 1988

I was working at 34 Kirkland late one night. They were painting all the offices. The furniture and file cabinets had all been pushed together in the center of the room. Jodi Picoult knocked at the door and asked to talk with a writer. She made her way through the clutter, fit herself into an empty chair and the desk lamp's circle of light. She had just graduated from Princeton and was now enrolled at Harvard. She was a novelist, and she hoped I might take a look at her novel, *Songs of the Humpback Whale*. I told her I wasn't a novelist, but I had attended the National Whale Symposium at Indiana University in 1975, where I heard the world premiere of George Crumb's *Vox Balaenae*. She had just moved to Cambridge, was starting a new program of study in education, didn't want her fiction writing to lose momentum. She convinced me to read the draft. I did, and we talked about it. Jodi published *Songs of the Humpback Whale* in 1992.

Visa

Mexico, 2000

It was absurd what we had to do to move Tomaz Salamun to Tuscaloosa as a visiting poet. His visa wasn't the right visa—he was a cultural attaché in New York City. I thought we could just go up to Birmingham to get the right visa, fill out a few forms, paperwork. But no. He had to fly out of the country, to Mexico, to get the new visa, the right visa, there, and re-enter the US with it. Why not Canada, I asked the guy whose only job for the university was to handle this kind of paperwork. Because Canada is the way old Soviet spies sneak in, he told me. He'll stand out surrounded by Mexicans. Tomaz, the absurdist that he was, loved all of it. The papers. The silly uniforms. The rubber-stamping. He loved how he didn't officially exist for a few days without a portfolio, and then he did but now all different.

Stock

New York, 1983

I never actually made it to the offices of *The New Yorker*. I came close. I called Lois Metzger from a payphone on the street. She worked as a typist there and said she would come down to meet me. Lois had been an orientation teacher a few years before at Johns Hopkins. We went to the Algonquin and caught up. I told her that my agent, Sallie Gouverneur, had worked at the magazine, reading for Ved Mehta, and that it had fallen to Veronica Geng to reject my stories that Sallie sent to the magazine. I owned stock in *The New Yorker*. It was publicly traded cheaply. The magazine struggled to attract advertising, and it maintained a large editorial staff. I knew this because I read closely the annual reports written in the style of "The Talk of the Town." I owned many shares that I sold two years later when S.I. Newhouse bought out the magazine. We walked back to *The New Yorker*'s building. I walked her to the door (there was a doorman, I think), and we said our goodbyes.

Riffs

Frostburg, 2014

I drove up through the mountains to Frostburg from Baltimore in a rental car, passing Civil War battlefields and steam train tourist railroads closed in the winter. I stayed in what was meant to look like a Swiss chalet motel, A-frame roofs and cedar shakes. I talked with a writing class and gave a reading in an old opera house movie theater downtown. At a nearby café, I met Stephen Dunn, who had recently retired from teaching and moved here. I told him I had used his book, *Riffs and Reciprocities*, in a prose poetry class I taught. We sat across the table from one another and reflected on what it felt like to be retired now, how Sundays felt all different, how you never retire from writing, how it is a good thing to talk in cafes with new people you've just met, also retired, and have poetic "organ recitals" as one declines on the top of a mountain. I left Frostburg and drove the switchbacks down to sea-level, crossing the bridge at Harpers Ferry, not knowing then I was a half-dozen years away from quitting myself.

Play Date

Boston, 1989

We watched our kids play or learn to play since they were very young and learning to do everything all at once. They were figuring how it all worked. This was in Tom Lux's backyard. Tom wore a Hawaiian shirt. Loud flowers. His daughter and my son, toddlers, got into things now at the drop of a hat. We all wore some kind of hat in the sun. We watched them closely. Without taking our eyes off them, Tom and I talked about dairy farms (Tom, the one he grew up on. Me, the one I worked on in Iowa before I came out to Boston), how dairy farmers are different, how they name their cows, how they can never leave because the herd must be milked day-in, day-out. It was, it is, its own kind of exhausted attention. We continued to watch the kids closely as they ran near the pool. We didn't drink, of course, but I'll never forget how Tom, deadpan sober, always referred to Glenfiddich as Glenfidget.

Molar

Montpelier, 2005

I often taught summers at the Vermont College of Fine Arts. The campus is on the top of a hill overlooking Montpelier, and at night, during the Leonid meteor shower, the shooting stars were always brilliant in the dark sky. A road ran steeply down the hill to the town. On one side, the road cut into the hill proper, the cut shored up by a high wall of massive granite blocks spackled with patches of concrete cement. I walked down the hill one day with Mary Ruefle so she could show me the tooth she had found: a molar, whole with the roots intact, erupting from the grouting. It was easy to miss. And it always took me a while to find it again when I climbed the hill or descended to the bookstore or for ice cream in town. It was so small, the tooth, and a bit decayed. The wall was massive and weathered. Mary and I looked at it for a long time as cars, their engines roaring, ground up the long hill behind us.

Gunkholing

The Chesapeake Bay, 2016

After lunch, John Barth (Jack) said we should go out gunkholing in the two-man kayak. Jack and Shelly lived outside of Chestertown but spent most of the time cruising Chesapeake Bay. We had crab cakes and beaten biscuits for lunch. On the water, we went in and out of inlets and coves and mouths of creeks. I said that I heard there was more shoreline in the Bay than the entire coastline of the USA. Well, yes and no, Jack said, since the Bay's shoreline would be part of the country's coast. "But I see what you mean." I'm from Indiana and had never been in a kayak or gone gunkholing before. I was in the front and Jack was in the back doing all the work.

Fiction

Baltimore, 1978

Edmund White introduced me to Richard Howard in the mailroom of Gilman Hall. They were on their way to Penn Station to take a train to New York City. It was a Thursday, and they were done teaching for the week. Ed told Richard, who had just published a book of poetic monologues in the voices of Henry James and Edith Wharton, that I was a fiction writer. "How nice for you," he said to me. "I will never have to think of you again then." Waving, they rushed through the door to catch their train.

Cut

Baltimore, 1979

John Irwin called me into his office. On his desk was a stack of papers, typed pages, over a foot high. Those are the stories of Stephen Dixon, John said. He wanted me to cut the pile down to a book he could publish with the press. There were many short stories. One was called "14 Stories," so I cut the stories down to 13 stories, including the story, calling it *14 Stories*. John published the book. I met Stephen when he came to Baltimore. Hopkins had hired him, and John asked me to show Stephen around. I told him I had read all those stories, cutting the book that was about to come out. He told me he wrote two or three stories a day in New York. He had hundreds of stories in circulation, placing a few each week. We walked around Homewood, through the campus into Wyman Park. I pointed out all the apartment buildings the university owned. We walked past the art museum, the equestrian statues of Lee and Jackson. I showed him the typos on the seated Poe sculpture that misquoted "The Raven."

Bread, Salt, Wine

Ames, 1984

We bought our first house. It was on 2nd Street in Ames. Almost the whole English Department faculty helped us move in. We didn't have a lot of stuff. We were just starting out. And it was quick work. We ordered pizza and had cold beers on ice in a metal washtub. People sat around on boxes and on chairs still on the little lawn. We were finishing up when Jane Smiley arrived. I had been on the committee that hired her. She said in the interview that she had plans to write all these different kinds of novels, and over time, she did. On 2nd Street, she pulled from the back of her station wagon a loaf of bread, a bottle of wine, and a box of salt, giving them to us and giving the housewarming speech from the movie *It's a Wonderful Life*.

B.

Battle Ground, 1998

I left Lafayette, driving out to Battle Ground to visit Patricia Henley, who lived there then. The town is bisected by the N&W tracks and the even older corridor of the Wabash and Erie Canal which traces the, very much older, still end moraine of the final glacier of the last ice age. I told Patricia I drove around there when I was in college looking for the town of B. in William Gass's story "In the Heart of the Heart of the Country." It wasn't Battle Ground, she said. It was Brookston up the road. I showed her the postcards I bought at Von's bookstore, the picture of a house in southern Indiana with a sign out front. The sign was printed with STORY and an arrow pointing right to the big number 5. Leaving town, I headed south through the tract of land where Tenskwatawa and the Shawnee had built Prophetstown. I stopped at the one-lane bridge over the Wabash, letting the northbound traffic cross first. From time to time since then, I've sent postcards to Patricia though she has, long ago, moved out of Battle Ground.

Available

Baltimore, 1992

In the lecture, Allen Grossman made clear that the lyric was no longer available to the American poet. Whitman's songs could not be sung in the 20th century or the next. After the Holocaust, he said, the mode must be narrative. Poets could not stop talking about the talk. At the reception, I mentioned that I had studied at Johns Hopkins ten years before. Grossman had just taken the Mellon Chair there, replacing Hugh Kenner. I had taken a class from Kenner, who had a hearing impairment and a pronounced lisp, and I remembered how he read aloud from memory William Carlos William's poem "The Sea Elephant." I tried to reproduce the sound he made when he made the "Blouaugh!" sound of the sea elephant. "Blouaugh!" I said. Not knowing, of course, what it was supposed to sound like only the way Kenner had made it sound all those years ago. Grossman laughed. At me? Or I didn't know what. "We've driven out the Nazis from Baltimore," he said.

Boxcar

Bloomington, 2011

After my reading at Boxcar Books, Ross Gay and I remembered Don Belton, who had been murdered two years before, the murderer's conviction pending. I met Don when we both taught a semester at Warren Wilson. Later, I arranged for him to teach a term in Tuscaloosa. He hired a national van line to move his books, furniture, and clothes to Alabama. I told Ross about the move. The van arrived before Don did. I supervised the unloading at the university-owned house. Fort Wayne is the headquarters of North American Van Lines. I grew up thinking it was The City of Blue Trucks. There were always blue trucks cycling through, packed with households looking to land. Indiana, the Crossroads of America. Don shipped a lot even though he had no permanent home then. Don arrived a few days later. I met him on the edge of town so he wouldn't get lost finding his way home. Don had found a home in Bloomington, Ross said. His books, papers, ephemera are all now stored in the Lilly Library. Then, Ross told me about the trees he was going to plant when the weather turned colder.

Confession

DeWitt, 2006

I told W. D. Snodgrass that his book, *Heart's Needle*, was the first poetry book I had ever bought. I was a student at Indiana University–Purdue University in Fort Wayne in Robert Novak's class in the spring of 1976. I confessed I read "April Inventory" every April since then. We did a reading together at Le Moyne College. It was the first time I had been back to Syracuse after I left the university there in 1996. He had taught at Syracuse, too, for ten years, 1958–68, at a time when English Departments still had classes in rhetoric, speech, and debate. I read first in what was now the standard singsong, voice rising as it nears the end of a line. It was strange and miraculous the way Snodgrass read, an old-fashioned platform speech, delivered stressing the beats, pounding the accents as he scanned with a booming voice, feet stamping. It was stunning to hear poetry delivered that way. I thought of an old scratchy record I heard once of Vachel Lindsay performing, not quite singing singing, a proto-rap. It was exhausting and Snodgrass, at the end, was exhausted.

Failure

Minneapolis, 2007

I wrote Charles Baxter right after I heard the news that the I-35 bridge had collapsed. I was watching the videotape of the bridge collapsing over and over on the television. Over a hundred vehicles had been on the bridge at the time of the collapse. It wasn't known if it was a bridge failure, some kind of sabotage, or an act of terror. I got in touch with Charlie to see if he and his family were okay and to gather news about people we knew in common. I knew, too, that his son, Daniel, had always been interested in civil engineering. I had met him years before in 1994 in Ann Arbor when Charlie lived there. We all talked then about trains and bridges and the famous rain of window glass that fell from the John Hancock building in Boston. Years later, Charlie told me that Daniel was sure he had seen something on the videotape, had even shared the information with the authorities. It was good to hear even amid such a dramatic and tragic failure that there had been a logic to it.

Graph

Swannanoa, 1991

At that conference where I heard Heather McHugh's lecture on fragments (later collected in the book, *Broken English*), I took notes on a tablet of yellow graph paper, the grid in blue ink. Heather noticed me taking notes, and said she admired the graph paper, how my block letters took up one square each. That might have been the time she had just discovered an anagram generator online. No, that was later. I had to leave on an early bus the next day, but not before I was able to slip a new, unused tablet of yellow graph paper, a gift, under her dorm room door.

Metamodernism

Syracuse, 1994

The Marxists in Textual Studies wouldn't speak to you because speech could not be critiqued. Mas'ud Zavarzadeh, whose office was across the hall from mine, played the radio while working. If I wanted him to turn the music down, I couldn't ask him directly. I would need to write a memo to that effect. I took to standing in the doorway, asking him questions, out loud, that he would ignore, knowing that I should put all my questions in writing. But after I kept asking, he would respond, especially when I asked about when and why he stopped writing about writers and began writing theoretical essays. I had read what he wrote about Donald Barthelme's fictions. He told me that he once believed that art and fiction could change the world, that literary fiction was a site of contestation. But now, he no longer believed that, and he no longer wished to create parasitic texts feeding on other texts. In 1975, he had coined the term "metamodernism" when he felt postmodernism had been exhausted. All the time we talked, I remember, the radio playing softly in the background.

Piano

Warren Wilson College, 1989

The first thing I learned about the residency at Warren Wilson was that Ellen Bryant Voight didn't sleep. I was a new faculty member and wound up, and I stayed awake, too, after everyone else had gone to their rooms. Ellen smiled and drank and told me stories and asked me about story writing as I was new and there to teach fiction writing. She'd play the out-of-tune piano, jazz standards mostly, and sing some. She founded the program, invented the concept of the low-residency model, and even after all these years she still fretted. She talked about Iowa and the other, mostly men, poets when she was there. I would finally drift off to my room, going to sleep with the soft piano sounds in the lobby still in my ear.

Retiring

Cambridge, 1985

Lewis Hyde told me about a lunch at the Harvard Faculty Club. If you were by yourself, they sat you at a large, shared table with other single diners. Lewis saw, as he was being escorted to the table, that three others were already seated there—John Kenneth Galbraith, Arthur Schlesinger, and B. F. Skinner. "I was about to be seated with these gray gruff intellectual giants," he told me. "What was I about to hear? What could I contribute?" Sitting down, he leaned into the group to introduce himself. Each greeted him politely before turning back to their ongoing conversation, which was, Lewis told me, about their retirement accounts of annuities and stock held by TIAA-Cref. Lewis told me another thing. His book, *The Gift*, about art's connection to the economics of gift giving and receiving and the building of gift communities, was highly successful. Everyone was reading the book, he told me. But people who had purchased *The Gift* liked it so much they then gave the book to a friend who then gave it away as well.

Steeping

Alta, 2013

There was still snow, ice really, on the mountain. In summer, the lifts don't lift, but the staff of Alta Lodge, after serving our lunch, climbed, all afternoon, to the peak for one fast run down the slope. Melanie Rae Thon and I watched them climb. At the base, we walked through the neighborhoods of empty condos and new construction. Melanie had driven me up from Salt Lake City, where she lived, to the writers' conference at the lodge, 8,600 feet, and returned mid-week to take a walk with me between the teaching. I remember nothing being level. Even going downhill felt like going up. The streets switched back and forth. The lodge was all stairs and landings. I told Melanie I found warnings in my room about altitude illness. A poem! We stopped, caught our breath, watching climbers climb higher toward the last ice clinging to the mountainside. As I think of it now, I should have told her about my *l'esprit de escalier* moment, saying what I say about what I should have said to my father and my mother, now gone, and all the other times we left behind.

Upside-Down

Chestertown, 1988

Robert Day was showing me around the Literary House on the campus of Washington College. The Lit House was home to a large letterpress room and bindery as well as classrooms, offices, and a public reading space where I was going to give a reading. The hallway walls were filled with finely designed printed broadsides and colorful posters, beautifully framed, advertising all the individual writers who had visited over the years. Walking slowly through the halls, we admired the gallery of famous names, and Bob related interesting anecdotes about each occasion. I noticed that every once in a while one of the posters was hung upside-down. After I had seen a number upside-down, I asked Bob why that was. He told me those had been the writers the students hadn't liked. I hoped then that my poster wouldn't end up so. Near the end of the tour, we came upon a poster hung not only upside-down (I imagined) but also back-to-front so all I could see was the brown backing paper. "The students really, really didn't like that one," he said. "You want to guess who it is?" And I did.

Tsantsa

Tuscaloosa, 2010

Escorting E.O. Wilson to the room in Smith Hall, the Natural History Museum, where he was going to read from his new novel, I mentioned that once there was a glass cabinet in this corridor that featured a shrunken human head. It had been displayed when I first moved to Tuscaloosa over a dozen years ago. It had been removed and replaced by a skeleton of a snake. "*Tsantsa*," Professor Wilson said, staring at the snake. "The Shurr people call them Tsantsa." He needed to use the restroom, and I pointed to the door nearby. I looked in the other cases at the other cabinets, read the little labels and the Latin captions. The reading, in the geological lecture hall, was a success. All the seats in the raked theater were filled. The novel was autobiographical about a boy growing up in southern Alabama, spending almost every moment in its swamps, looking closely, of course, at ants.

Squeegee

Ames, 1985

Mark Strand and I watched an art student pull a silk screen broadside of one of his poems. The letters were the last thing to be printed. The fine paper being used had already been randomly stained with horizontal blobs of pastel colors in such a way that no two were alike. The student asked Strand if he would like to try. He pulled the squeegee expertly, the black ink thinning out over the silk. I pulled one too. This was the easy part, I thought, the squeak the squeegee made going slowly over the silk, the words appearing magically below as you pull the ink along. Later, when we went back, the sheets had been hung up to dry like laundry. Strand signed and numbered each one over the number of the whole run. There were artist's proofs as well that had interesting mistakes. He took home one of those. Some of the numbered sheets were given away at the reading. The rest were sold to raise money for *Poet & Critic*, the journal I edited. There was something so satisfying, he said, about writing with a squeegee.

Real Estate

Syracuse, 1994

Jonathan Franzen was in Syracuse visiting David Foster Wallace. Jonathan was thinking about moving to Syracuse, getting out of New York where the rent and real estate had gone mad. Could I drive them around? I had a new car, a Corolla station wagon. I drove them to Syracuse China's seconds shop. Every piece had at least one interesting mistake. I showed them Lake Onondaga, then the most polluted lake in the world. There was a big mall nearby. I drove by the zoo. In Manlius, at the Stickley factory, I showed them the swimming swans in the nearby pond. I drove around the drumlin hills to see the four-square houses, the Dutch colonial houses, many empty and going for a song. I ended up at the bungalow on Maryland Avenue where Raymond Carver and Tess Gallagher had lived. I thought about buying it when I moved to Syracuse, but its history had put a premium on the price. In the new car again, I told them that I was still breaking it in. The dealer said, I told them, that if Lexus made a station wagon, this would be it.

Not Lobster

Gorham, 1986

It was my first vacation in Maine where Theresa had gone to college. She had lived in Portland and attended the University of Southern Maine, where Kenneth Rosen taught a poetry workshop. She was excited about showing me Maine. Lobster, she told me, was not Maine's special dish. The Italian sandwich was. We drove to The Stonecoast Summer Writing Conference Ken ran in Gorham to hear Andre Dubus read. We got there early to get a good seat and sat next to Alyson Hagy, who was assisting in Robley Wilson, Jr.'s workshop. We knew Rob from Iowa, but it was our first time meeting Alyson. Rob said something mysterious. "Who did you come here to see?" We were confused, thought we had gotten the dates wrong or the place. It turned out that Andre Dubus had been seriously injured the day before in a car accident. We hadn't known. It is strange still, looking back on it. Why had Rob made us guess what was happening? We continued "Down East," driving to Freeport to see The Desert of Maine the next day.

Meatless

Red Line, 1987

I was inbound on the Red Line train with Christopher Leland, a Braintree train, heading to Dorchester where Chris lived. Leaving Central Square's underground station, I told him about the day I moved into Cambridge and ordered a veggie sub in a shop in Central Square. While waiting, I looked out the window at this strange new world, Central Square. "Yo, Meatless!" the counterman yelled at me, "You want cheese on that?" "Welcome to Cambridge," Chris said then. There was the Harvard Donut Shop that didn't sell donuts, but muffins, he said, muffins the size of small animal brains. We were sitting on the long bench that ran the length of the car between the doors, looking at our reflections in the window opposite. Just before the train emerged after the Kendall/MIT stop, and before it would stall halfway across Longfellow Bridge, Chris pointed at the ghostly images caught in the window on the other side of the car. "What are you looking at?" he asked them. And then said to me, "Can you believe these guys?"

Grades

Flagstaff, 2013

I had a drink with Pam Houston in the country club bar. There was a big north-facing window that looked out over the open course. The sky was smoky from uncontrolled fires we couldn't see. We couldn't see the Grand Canyon, but it was out there somewhere, too. Nicole Walker had invited us to town for a book fair. The reception at the country club was for the authors, publishers, and patrons. I had just had an argument with someone at the bar before Pam arrived, and I told her about it. It concerned grading writing, grading stories, and grading poems. I had to give grades, but I always gave all A's. This guy thought that plumb crazy, etc. "You're not critical at all!" he said. I told him I wasn't a critic, but a writer myself, and had no idea what constituted the difference, when it came to writing, between an A minus or a B plus. Pam and I looked out the window. I told her I lived in a house that looked out over an abandoned country club going to ruin. Then I asked her to grade the story I just told her. And she did.

Evidence

Port Townsend, 1993

Before reading from her book of poems, *Flash Paper*, Theresa lit a piece of flash paper on fire. It sparked, burst into flame, and disappeared. In Baltimore, flash paper was illegal. Bookies there used the treated paper to record their bets and burn the evidence if need be, leaving nothing, not even ashes, she said. Her father had been a bookie in Baltimore. She read in the theater on the old army base where the Centrum Writing Conference was held. William Stafford was in the audience. He would die later that year. He famously wrote every day. In his workshops, he always said one should neither praise nor blame, and when writers came to him saying they were blocked, he said they should lower their standards. That night at his reading, he began by reminding us how long he'd lived but how there was always something new. And then he mentioned Theresa's flash paper demonstration and her reading. Theresa, back in the barrack with Sam, missed his reading. I told her about the reading and how she had impressed William Stafford at hers.

Come Back

Syracuse, 1996

Safiya Henderson-Holmes and I co-taught a class that introduced a half-dozen Black poets, living writers, to a class of fifty Syracuse freshmen. The students wanted to know why all the blurbs said that the poets were "angry." Safiya and I laughed. Right before I moved away, I waited in the recovery room with her after her second surgery. I told a doctor friend what kind of tumors she had had removed, and he winced, "Oh, they come back ..." Safiya lived in a grand apartment carved out of Gustav Stickley's Arts & Crafts house, all quarter-sawn oak and leaded windows, where we laughed about how angry she was.

Boston or Baltimore

Fort Wayne, 1978

B ack then, in 1978, there were only a handful of MFA grad schools. Boston University and Johns Hopkins weren't even MFA programs. They gave out MAs in creative writing. I applied to nine or ten programs. I got into Hopkins, and George Starbuck called me from Boston with an offer. I was a bit overwhelmed. I'd never been out of Indiana, really, and I told him that. "You don't want to go to Hopkins," he said. "Baltimore is the world's largest small town." I thought about that. And I thought a big small town sounded right for me. Sixteen years later, I was a professor, and I was moving to teach at the University of Alabama in Tuscaloosa. A week before I arrived, George Starbuck, who had retired there, died in that small, small town I was now moving to.

92nd

New York, 1977

We thought we wouldn't make it in time. A group of us, John Barth's students, piled into Jay Brandon's car, drove up from Baltimore to see Barth read with Donald Barthelme at the 92nd Street Y. As the sun set, the dramatic flames shooting from the refineries of New Jersey became pronounced. We arrived, just in time, and found seats in the back of the crowded room. Barth read "Night Sea Journey" again. I had seen him read it before, and I would see him read it again. Light bounced off his bald head as he bowed at the end. Barthelme read a new story, "Cortez and Montezuma," that would be published later that year in *The New Yorker* on my birthday. Afterward, we all went backstage. Jack introduced his students to Don, and Don introduced his students to Jack. I shook Donald Barthelme's hand. The students then introduced themselves to each other. We stayed that night in an apartment nearby, my student's family's apartment, sleeping on couches, in chairs, and on the floor. Stuart Davidson, my student, went on to be a notable trial attorney in Philadelphia.

Blue Rain

Syracuse, 1991

I had just started teaching at Syracuse, and one day, a first-year undergraduate student walked into my office wanting an independent study in poetry. There was an intro class I told him. He said both of his parents were poets. He felt he was beyond intro. Adam Cohen was his name. We talked more about poetry and poets and then about Greece. Suddenly, I thought to ask, "Cohen?" I asked. "Your father is Famous Blue Raincoat Cohen?" "Yes," he answered. I had been hired as a prose writer. I was still learning the ropes there, but I signed him up for an independent study class in poetry. He said, "Cool."

Coincidental

New York, 1983

My book, *Alive and Dead in Indiana*, might not be published. The lawyers at Knopf cut several stories, citing I had characters invading the privacy of real people. I learned dead characters or famous ones had no right to privacy, I learned. But others, like James Dean's high school drama teacher, did. "Can you prove that she said this?" the lawyers asked. No, I had made it up. "Cut it," they said, "or get her permission." I was telling all of this to Amy Hempel in a bar somewhere in New York. We shared an editor, and her book, *Reasons to Live*, would come out the year after mine. I couldn't talk with our editor. His forthcoming book used real people as fictional characters too. I learned from the lawyers that the inoculation clause—"This is a work of fiction. Any resemblance to actual persons, living or dead, is purely coincidental"—didn't work. Amy reassured me. Things would work out. And they did. Later, in another bar in Indiana, I read Mrs. Nall, the story "she" narrated. "It is all lies," she said, but gave me permission, signed on a cocktail napkin, anyway.

Epoch

Washington, D.C., 2011

In the lobby outside the Shoreham Hotel's ballroom, Juan Reyes let me know that he had just heard Junot Diaz's AWP session inside the ballroom where he mentioned me by name. Junot gave a reading and was answering audience questions. Someone asked about his, Junot's, influences, and he, Junot, asked if anyone knew Michael Martone. Juan said that he, Juan, let out a little shout. "Yeah," Juan said Junot said, "I read Martone's stories when I was reading for *Epoch* at Cornell." "Yeah," he said, "They're all set in Indiana, always in Indiana." And Juan said Junot said, "I wanted to do that, too, have a place, have people in my stories." I wasn't surprised to hear this. Junot had shared that with me earlier. Yes, I told him, Indiana is my own special island. But it must have been a surprise to everyone listening to Junot in the Shoreham Hotel Ballroom.

Godzilla

Columbus, 1985

On the second try, I made it to Ohio to do a reading at the Thurber House in Columbus. A snowstorm grounded my first attempt. I got stuck at the TWA hub in St. Louis. I called Michael Rosen, the literary director then at the Thurber House who asked, "Where are you?" When I finally made it there, we had some extra time after the event. So, Michael took me to see the new Godzilla movie, *Return of Godzilla*. We are about the same age. He grew up in Ohio, and I grew up, not far away, in Indiana. We found we had a lot in common. We both had been looking forward to the return of Godzilla, and we especially liked the part where Godzilla, the Godzilla that is a Godzilla suit worn by an actor, destroys the toy infrastructure of Tokyo, ripping through the sparking power lines, elbowing the tall buildings, and stomping on the elevated railway tracks. We both agreed, later, that that was always the best part of a Godzilla movie.

Lowest Common
Denominator

Portland, 2006

I was in Portland for the Writers on the Edge Conference, and wherever I went to eat—a truck on the street, a cheap diner, a fancy sit-down place—they all had a Caprese salad on the menu. All the Caprese salads all listed the same ingredients too—fresh Buffalo mozzarella, sweet basil, and heirloom tomatoes, always heirloom tomatoes. I mentioned I noticed that every place in Portland seemed to carry a Caprese salad with heirloom tomatoes to Lidia Yuknavitch, who laughed and called the Caprese salad Portland's lowest common denominator food. It didn't matter how nice or nasty, everyone had a Caprese salad with Buffalo mozzarella and heirloom tomatoes. She asked what Tuscaloosa's lowest common denominator food would be. I thought about it, and I finally settled on Buffalo chicken wings with blue cheese dressing.

Normal

Normal, 1999

I stayed in Normal where Doug Hesse and Becky Bradway lived. Doug taught at Illinois State, and Becky taught at Milliken in nearby Decatur. She had invited me to read there, and I did. I stayed an extra day to have lunch with David Foster Wallace who had just started teaching in Normal. We had met a few years before when we were both in Syracuse. I was teaching there, and David had just gotten the job in Normal. Over lunches, we'd talk about teaching and writing and about teaching writing. Now that I was in Normal, we met to talk about how things were going. After lunch, we drove around town, a very Midwestern thing to do. I'm from Indiana and David had grew up in Urbana-Champaign, not far away. I had published an essay of his about playing tennis in an anthology I edited called *Townships*. As we drove around, he showed me the tennis courts of Normal. I wanted to see the original Steak 'n Shake. I think we saw the headquarters of State Farm Insurance Company, but I can't be sure now.

Reach

Syracuse, 1992

It was a full house to hear Robert Stone read from his new novel, *Outerbridge Reach*, and his patter before the reading went on a long time—solo circumnavigation sailing, the races he had read about, being lost at sea. He then read a paragraph from the book and sat down. It was the shortest reading I have ever attended. We all sat there about as long as the reading had taken, not sure if it was over, and then we left.

Spoon

Minneapolis, 2006

Robin Hemley travels so much doing readings, classes, conferences, and consultations that he has an enormous amount of airline miles. We were together at the Minneapolis airport, waiting for flights home, after we taught together at a conference at St. Olaf College in Northfield. Because he was a platinum member of Northwest's frequent flyers club, he could use the grand first-class lounge in the airline's major hub, and he was able to take a guest: me. It was everything I imagined. Overstuffed chairs and couches, thick carpets, televisions tuned to different channels, buffet tables with mixed nuts and dried fruit, chafing dishes of hors d'oeuvres, cutting boards of crackers and cheese, and metal flatware (though the knives were still plastic) stamped with the NWA's logo on the handles. I thanked Robin many times as we left to go to our different departure gates. I stole a spoon. I have it still. I use it every morning to eat my breakfast yogurt.

Trick or Treat

Boston, 1989

We were in the Year of the Great Forgetting, our firstborn having just been born. We'd met Rosanna Warren ten years before in Baltimore. Now, it was Halloween, and Rosanna was living in Boston too, and had a baby as well, and said we should come over and bring the baby. I think I remember it was raining that night, and we were lost and late, and when we found the house, the porch light was off, and when Rosanna came to the door, it took a while, she said, because she thought we were trick or treaters and she had forgotten to get candy, and she had forgotten about the invitation, and she was shocked to see us there on the porch in the rain. We all had cheese and crackers, and the babies were fussy, and we sat quietly when the doorbell rang.

Traps

Baltimore, 1978

The only thing we talked about was the cockroaches of Baltimore. Cockroaches began showing up in the poems and stories being considered in the seminars. The program lasted only one year. Not even a year, really, but nine months, the school year. Not even nine months as the thesis had to be finished by February so it could be typed and formatted perfectly. We talked more about cockroaches than we did about our poems it seemed. Once, I opened a cupboard door and the back of the door came alive, a swarm of cockroaches. Elizabeth Spires was from Circleville, Ohio, famous for its pumpkins. Her father was an exterminator. She knew about cockroaches, and her father sent new glue traps. You could look inside and see the long antennae of the mired insect waving slowly back and forth. Beth was the only one of us that had a new IBM Selectric typewriter. It had a tiny memory that allowed the machine to erase a mistake. We talked about the cockroaches in Beth's traps and her typewriter.

Wind

Northfield, 2008

I grew my hair out, not cutting it at all, during the George W. Bush administration. I taught a weeklong workshop that summer at St. Olaf College, sleeping in a hilltop dorm next to a giant wind turbine that turned constantly. Carleton College across town had an identical wind turbine turning on another hill. It was like they were signaling to each other. I called Louise Erdrich who lives in Minneapolis. I had a little flip phone. I told her I wouldn't be able to see her, but that I was in Northfield. I had a break between things and was saying hello. She was at home, she said, but near her computer. She told me that St. Olaf's had a "webcam." This was something new then, webcams, and she directed me where to find one. I went outside on the road near my dorm. I found the camera in the eaves of a nearby hall and looked up at it. The wind turbine was turning slowly behind me in the distance. I waved at the camera, the phone at my ear. "Your hair," Louise said, "it's so long."

Spade

Cambridge, 1990

Everyone thinks Harvard University is rich, but it is cheap when it comes to phones. My office at 34 Kirkland Street was next to Seamus Heaney's, and we shared a party line that rang all the time. The calls were almost always for him from all over the world. I took messages, and when he returned, we would have lunch in his office to review them. We would also talk about gardens and how we missed having one in the city. When I left to take a new job in a city where I could have a garden, Seamus gave me a garden spade with a ribbon around its handle which is, after all these years and many gardens, still there, hanging by a few threads.

RDC

Syracuse, 1995

We had finished lunch at a nice restaurant in Armory Square and sat around talking about nothing, really. The Square was being renovated. Restaurants and bars, galleries and gift shops were moving into old warehouses and vacant wholesale stores. The restaurant's big windows looked out over to the brick armory encrusted with scaffolding. Behind it, on the raised railway roadbed, a silver RDC crept up to a makeshift platform. Joyce Carol Oates asked us what was going on. I told her that it was an RDC, a Rail Diesel Car, a self-propelled passenger car. It was an experiment, I said, the car ran back and forth from Syracuse's campus, up on its hill, through Armory Square out to the Carousel Mall near Lake Onondaga. Carousel Mall as an attraction had an old-fashioned merry-go-round, I told her. She hadn't been out there, she said, as the RDC sounded its horn and drifted out of the station, but would have to go.

No Pants

Tuscaloosa, 2014

We missed seeing Rick Moody and Laurel Nakadate when they were in Tuscaloosa. They were on their way to Iowa. Iowa was where we first knew Laurel, who is the daughter of a colleague of mine, Neil Nakadate, when I taught there thirty years before. It was the end of the fall semester. We had already headed north, but the campus was still busy with students finishing up the term or remaining in town for winter graduation ceremonies. We knew this because later they asked us what it was exactly the young women students were wearing. It looked, they said, as if none of them were wearing pants. Tuscaloosa is warm enough in December to still wear shorts, we told them, and the women students wear short-short Nike running shorts that are hidden under extra-long sweatshirts or long-sleeve tees. It creates the appearance that that is all they are wearing—the sweatshirts, long-sleeve tees—and nothing else. "We thought it was some kind of tradition," they said, "or a uniform specific to the South." They would always remember their visit as "No-Pants December."

Lichen

Asheville, 1994

I never learned to drink coffee and never had a cup of coffee until that summer in Asheville. We were sitting outdoors at a coffee shop on Pack Square. I was looking to order my usual at a coffee shop, a lemonade or sparkling water. Andrea Barrett could not believe I had never had a coffee. I told her about never learning to drink it in college, and about not really liking hot drinks. She proposed an experiment. Try a coffee. I can't remember why I said okay, but I said okay. I even ordered an espresso. Andrea, along with Debra Spark and Judith Grossman, watched me as I sipped. I had never felt my heart before. And I told them that: I was feeling my heart for the first time. Later, after I returned home, Andrea sent me a package of smooth stone fragments, chips covered with bright lichen, and a note that said these were an interesting group of crustose lichen called "script" lichens *Graphis scripta* and have spore structures that look like writing. "*The lirellae look like scribbles on the thallus . . .*," said the handwritten note.

Giants

Ann Arbor, 2004

I was in Ann Arbor to see the band They Might Be Giants. I arrived early so I could go downtown and browse in the famous bookstores of Ann Arbor. The original Borders was still there and open then. In Shaman Drum, I ran into Brian Evenson browsing a Borges book. We agreed the meeting was very Borgesian. I told him I was in town for the They Might Be Giants concert that night. We talked about the Giants and bookstores, how we loved them. I had worked in one, and I think Brian said he had too. They were beginning to disappear. Borders, which had expanded from Ann Arbor all around the country and overseas, had gobbled them up. In the not-too-distant future, Borders, too, would be gone. We didn't know it then, but Shaman Drum would close in five years. I bought one of Brian's books there, in Shaman Drum, so he could sign it then and there. And he did.

Dumb

Baltimore, 1978

Grace Paley didn't like that I used the word "mothering" in the question I asked her. "Don't use 'mother' as a verb ever." I don't think I have ever used it as a verb since. She was talking to a class of first-time teachers. I was one of them. We were "teaching" one of her books, *Enormous Changes at the Last Minute*. I asked another dumb question, something like "What's my job as a teacher?" "Your job," she said, "is to make your students dumb again."

Coats

Iowa, 1984

It was December in Iowa, and the sky was lowering, and I was out in the country with Wendell Berry looking for Maury Telleen's farm outside Waverly. Wendell knew Maury through *Draft Horse Journal*. Wendell wanted to see Maury and the Percherons he kept. I had on a new canvas barn coat, and Wendell said, "Nice coat." In the gloaming, it began to spit snow, and flurries then whipped up by the wind. In the cloud of snow, the massive clouds of horses, mares, and yearlings, stood motionless, steaming in the snow, dark gray like their thick new coats.

Blue Hair

Cambridge, 1987

That night I read "Blue Hair," an anecdote, taken from something I had read recently in the *Boston Globe* about the woman whose long, straight hair was used to make the crosshairs in the famous Norden bombsights. I hadn't known that they used real hair as crosshairs. Bill Knott read after me. I had been the warm-up act for him in his hometown. This was the first time I had given a reading in Cambridge. The large crowd in Adams House was focused on Bill Knott, of course. He read very short poems very quickly that were very funny and threw the pages on the ground after he read from them. The poems went off like hand grenades, one after the other. I watched Marie Howe and Mary Karr, who were sitting in the front row, burst into laughter after each one of his poems landed.

Corny

Warren Wilson, 1989

The three of us—Richard Russo, C.J. Hribal, and I—had rooms in the dorm next door to the main one. It was snowing, and we were walking in single file across the lawn through the snow. Someone called us the "Corn Boys" and it stuck. Rick was teaching in Illinois. C.J. was from Wisconsin. And even though I was living in Massachusetts, I wrote about Indiana. We must have looked Midwestern to our amused colleagues. Rick always gave the last lecture at the residency, writing it during the week and in his talk responding to the other lectures and classes that had gone before. It was remarkable. The next time we were together, I gave them each a cheap tin pin in the shape of a corncob to wear on our winter coats.

Intersection

Baltimore, 2015

Z Z Packer and I had breakfast in a place on Charles Street that overlooked a parking lot where the Peabody Bookshop and Beer Stube once was, a hangout of Mencken. ZZ and I had both attended the Writing Seminars, years apart, and were back in town to celebrate the opening of an exhibition of our retired teacher's ephemera at the Peabody Library. We compared our two Baltimores. I told her about Abe Sherman's Bookstore, also gone, and the Owl Bar at the Belvedere where Scott and Zelda drank. Of course, now Baltimore was the Baltimore of *The Wire*. But the row houses were still the row houses, rows and rows of row houses. She didn't remember the Inner Harbor smelling of spices when McCormick's factory still operated at the intersection of Pratt and Light. In the parking lot across Charles, an Arabber's pony cart was setting up to sell produce from the Eastern Shore. After we talked about all the people we knew in common and the places we had both been but not at the same time, it was time to go, and off we went.

Hotbed

Tuscaloosa, 2004

I wrote to T. C. Boyle. I had a question about something I read in his new book, *The Inner Circle*, a novel set in Bloomington, Indiana, and involving Alfred Kinsey, the sexologist, and his inner circle of researchers. Early in the book, a minor character is introduced with the name of "Martone." I wrote to T. C. Boyle about that. I thought it might have been a nod my way as two decades before *The Inner Circle* appeared, I wrote and published a story called "Alfred Kinsey, Alone after an Interview, Dreams of Indiana." In the email, I asked T. C. Boyle if that was maybe the case. He wrote back right away, saying no, he used the name of a childhood friend (he was born and raised in Peekskill, New York) and had never read my story but would try to read it soon. Martone is not that common a name, I thought. I did a cursory search online and discovered Peekskill is a hotbed of Martones—Martone & O'Toole Appraisal Company, Martone Realty, Martone Auto Collision—and we are all probably related one way or the other.

Waffles

Tallahassee, 2001

I spent the night in Robert Olen Butler's writing studio that had a new satellite television hook-up. It had been tuned to the Fukuoka Grand Sumo Tournament, just finished in November. In the house, there was a huge collection of hot sauces in the kitchen and a gallery of shoes, under glass, in the dining room. In the morning, he wanted to take me to this place for waffles. We sped along a busy four-lane highway in his convertible, the top down. This was Florida in winter. Bob, a good tour guide, narrated us through the abundant points of interest along the way. We sped by a cowering dog in the grassy median strip, obviously attempting to get across the road through the rushing traffic. Bob immediately pulled over, skidding to a stop, and bolted out of the car to rescue the animal. We never made it to the waffle place. We went to look for the dog's owner and home.

Beat

Black Mountain, 1990

I had a drink once with Joyce Johnson in a sleepy Black Mountain bar long after that college closed, though what was left of it was still haunted. We were teaching down the road at Warren Wilson in Swannanoa. I didn't know then that she had been Jack Kerouac's lover. We had team-taught a workshop, considering drafts of chapters from novels. Later, I would read her memoir, *Minor Characters*, and teach it in a class called "Construction of Authorship" paired with *On the Road*. I wish I'd known then in Black Mountain. I had, still have, so many questions about the Beats, about the drinking, about the remembering.

Meat and Three

Tuscaloosa, 2004

Lydia Davis and I, sitting in the bar of the Cypress Inn, looked out the big windows and watched a towboat push a coal barge down the Black Warrior River. I pointed out the rustic signs tacked to the pine tree on the riverbank, recording the various high-water marks of past floods. The Cypress Inn was a "fancy" restaurant, but it was nothing more than an upscale "meat and three," ubiquitous southern diner that serves a meat and three vegetable side dishes. "It is really more like a meat and meat and meat and meat," I told her, as all the vegetables were cooked with bacon fat and/or ham hocks. "Lard, there is a lot of lard." The greens, the beans, creamed corn, the hoppin' john. "What's hoppin' john?" she wanted to know. And I told her.

Names

Cambridge, 1987

No one there at the Blacksmith House poetry reading can remember why Franz Wright was late that night or what he actually said after being introduced. He made his way up front to read after Theresa Pappas had finished reading her poems. He might have thanked her, praised the poems or apologized for being late, I can't remember. But I do remember he called Theresa "Irene" instead of Theresa and then began his (Franz's, not Richard's) reading.

Prose

Syracuse, 1992

I introduced Francine Prose when she came to read at Syracuse, part of the Raymond Carver Reading Series. In the introduction, I said the scope and abundance of her work should remind us of Charles Dickens. She had a Dickensian eye for status detail and social dynamics, and rendered a rich, attractive bleakness. Outside there had been an ice storm, and I had driven her to the reading through an early darkness. Syracuse suffers from the lake effect ceiling of clouds and is in the center of what historians call The Burned-Over District. Her reading was a big success and was well attended, even though there had been an ice storm that day and there was the usual gloom that followed us out into the night. And later, she sent a thank you note to me, typed on the back of a C.T. Art Color-Tone linen postcard that depicted the old Art Deco New York Central depot in soft pastel colors.

Daylilies

New Harmony, 1991

Roxana Robinson and I watched Jane Owen, in her signa-ture floppy- brimmed hat, weed a huge drift of daylilies, a bank outside the Inn in New Harmony. We were there for the Ropewalk Writers Retreat, teaching workshops in the morning. In the afternoon the writers were encouraged to retreat—write or just meander around the restored village, the site of two failed 19th-century utopias. Jane Owen, an oil heiress, restored the ruin of the town and commissioned Philip Johnson and Richard Meier, nurtured gardens and golden rain trees. Roxana had never taught before and sat in on my workshop, but after class, we talked about the gardens. I had just started a garden in Syracuse and planted Rosa rugosa and peonies and was looking for advice from Roxana, who tended her own long-established lovely garden. I told her about the waste of buckwheat hulls I got from an old mill in New York to use as mulch, gunmetal gray, and feathery. Mostly, I just listened to Roxana talk with Jane about the gardens, sitting in a golf cart not far from the pine straw-carpeted park where Paul Tillich's ashes were interred.

Tilth

Seattle, 2007

After my reading, David Shields and Maya Sonenberg took me to a restaurant called Tilth. Then, it was a newly opened, pioneering organic restaurant that featured fresh farm-to-table, locally sourced fare. The meal was prix fixe, and all the courses as they were served were introduced by the server who narrated the life and setting of the ingredients, the process of how the produce had been picked and transformed, cooked, and plated. I remember one dish was a carrot foam and the detail that the carrot had been harvested that morning from a field on a fork of a river whose name I've forgotten. At every other table, other servers were telling their tables about the food being served. The room, a converted living room of a house, murmured. Maya, David, and I listened intently to our server's litanies while the others became a kind of ambient background, even as the carrot foam lost its effervescence.

Townships

Cambridge, 1989

Townships, Jim Harrison was telling me over the phone, are still important here in Michigan. I was glad to hear it as I had come up with this idea for an essay anthology: Midwestern writers writing about their particular townships. It was a stretch, a tortured metaphor. The whole country outside the original 13 states had been surveyed into this imaginary grid of six-mile by six-mile squares. But only in the Midwest, my thesis went, did the grid "take." See that quilted pattern below when you fly over the flyover states? The Midwest! I contacted dozens of writers. Many had never heard of townships, let alone the name of theirs. But Jim Harrison knew. He was interested and would try to rig something together. We left it at that. I didn't have any money to pay the contributors. I thought this intriguing prompt was rewarding enough. The writers could use their essays in their own books. It didn't work out with Jim. An assistant later said he said I was nuts to think anyone would write anything without getting paid. He wasn't wrong.

Copies

Monroeville, 1998

I asked Brad Watson how he liked Harvard and Cambridge. He had just moved there as a Briggs-Copeland Lecturer on Fiction. Everyone has a title there, I told him. I had had the same job a decade before. The work-study student put his name and PRECEPTOR OF XEROGRAPHY on the door of the copier closet. We were in Monroeville for the Alabama Literary Festival. His book, *The Last Days of the Dog-Men*, was new. We were to talk about writing about "Place," here in the place where Harper Lee and Truman wrote. "Place" meant Monroeville. After our session, there was a reception. Shrimp and cheese grits, barbeque, chess pie, and sweet tea. Brad found it strange, Harvard, in the way it rubbed up against a working-class town, another place with its own accent, its own way of naming, its copy of copies.

Paris

Fort Wayne, 1976

George Plimpton's lecture at Indiana University-Purdue University was about "participatory journalism" and his books reporting on professional baseball, football, and golf. He said he was thinking about doing a book on professional hockey. And later he did. He mused on the word "amateur" and how it was connected to the word "love." Most of the audience had no idea that he was also the editor of *The Paris Review.* They were there for the anecdotes about sports and to hear about being in the movies or cast on a television show. We were encouraged to send written questions up to him. At the end of the talk, he went through index cards, answering the questions. My question asked if he would allow me to edit one issue of *The Paris Review* so that I could write about the experience later. He read the question aloud, looked up, and gazed at the audience. I raised my hand, waving. "Moving on . . ." was all he said and moved on to the next question.

Oxygen

Tuscaloosa, 2008

On the phone was Barry Hannah, calling from Oxford, saying, "Michael, I believe I'm dying. Would it be possible," he wanted to know, "if I could arrange a final reading in Tuscaloosa?" I arranged it, the reading, at the Bama downtown, a Depression Era theater made to look like a Moorish courtyard with fake stars twinkling on the dark blue ceiling. It was packed with people who never came to readings. Barry recalled the arrows he shot at his ex-wife's front door, and tennis at the Country Club. He didn't have to mention shooting holes in his MG Midget's floorboard after forgetting to put the top up overnight. He started reading "Tuscaloosa," and people got up to leave. Earlier, walking into the reading, I'd been behind Barry and a clutch of old, now sober, colleagues. Barry's driver and assistant pulled a holster out of his shoulder bag, smiling at me as he unzipped it. "You thought it was a gun, didn't you?" he said. I did. But it wasn't. It was the fixings, tubes, and mask, for Barry's oxygen concentrator. He needed to catch his breath before he began.

Chair

Tuscaloosa, 2000

I think I owned Richard Yates's chair. It was a cheap, Danish Modern thing, a sling of leather suspended between slender sticks of blond wood. The provenance was sketchy. Yates ended up living (and dying) in Tuscaloosa, having never left after being invited to the University of Alabama as a Coal Royalty Visiting Writer. Hitting a bottom after that, he had nowhere else to go. He died in 1992, four years before I arrived. Then, the local literary magazine, *Black Warrior Review*, held an annual auction to raise money, offering a variety of exotic items that were bid upon, an excuse to donate money while drinking at a bar. Richard Yates's chair was one such lot. The next year I would donate it back to auction and then bid on it again, winning sometimes, sometimes not. No one knew, really, if it was or was not the chair salvaged from his tiny studio apartment (now also long gone) after he died. Mid-century modern furniture never really caught on in Tuscaloosa, where tastes ran more to the neoclassical and antebellum. It was a tortured, beat-up contraption, more sculpture than chair.

Vasovagal

Philadelphia, 2014

I read with Samuel Delany at the Mutter Museum in Philadelphia. It was after hours. The galleries were closed and dark. Still, there were large pictures of anatomical specimens—skeletons, organs, antique medical instruments—on the walls behind the podium where he was reading. There were locked glass cabinets—cross sections of brains, catalogues of human skulls—all around the auditorium. It was raining and gloomy outside. For as long as I can remember I have suffered from vasovagal response. I get light-headed, even faint—syncope—not so much at the sight of blood or bone, viscera or carnage, but by hearing or reading those words, especially Latinates, about the body. *Contusion* instead of bruise. *Laceration* not cut. *Syncope* makes me syncope. Not the specimens and diagrams that get to me but the labels labeling. However, that night the words that were working were Delany's as he read. That a word, words could do this to me. A lexicon's autopsy of an autopsy, an etymological surgery performed in a gothic surgical theater, the glass cabinets of a Philadelphia Wunderkammer. Before I knew it, I was out.

Star

Tuscaloosa, 2010

Neil Gaiman loved the skeleton of the whale, floating overhead in the big gallery of the Natural History Museum. Earlier he had told me about going to China where now they wanted to export more than just inexpensive copies of consumer products. They wanted to see how they could copy humans who imagine things completely new. New products, new art, new stories. "It was," he said, "as if he was being reverse-engineered!" I showed him the display in the corner. The hefty rock from Sylacauga is called the Hodges meteorite because a fragment struck Ann Fowler Hodges while she napped. It is the only known time a star struck a living human. "That gives me an idea," he said.

Prozac

Indianapolis, 1996

I was a student at Butler in the 70s and hated every minute. The carillon there played a clunky rendition of "Back Home Again in Indiana." Walking across the gloomy campus, clouds pressing down overhead, I'd whisper with the tolling: Back home again in Indiana where the sun refuses to shine. Indianapolis was Naptown then. Its downtown is nothing but rust-stained war monuments and mausoleums, insurance companies, and empty parking lots. Its beltway always filled with trucks and cars going nowhere slowly. Years later, Susan Neville invited me to read at Butler. She met me at my flight's gate. You could do that then. Walking to the car, I saw a new skyline in the distance. She drove me downtown on the new expressway to a new hotel in the old but newly renovated Union Station. There was a new arena, a new stadium. The one high-rise bank building had been eclipsed by higher-rising bank buildings. The sun, the sun was out, and the sky was sky-blue. "Susan," I exclaimed, "what the hell happened?" She paused, rounding a southside curve. The Eli Lilly complex hove into view. "Prozac," was all she said.

Acknowledgments

Turns out, a Table Talk is a subspecies of the memoir in the genre of nonfiction. Who knew? Martin Luther could be said to have kicked it off, his talk at table recorded by a lesser, no name writer, a Johannes Mathesius, in the 16th Century. Other Table Talks followed. Milton, Johnson, Goethe, Coleridge, Pushkin, Emerson, Shaw, Auden. I had no idea when, four years ago, I retired after forty years of teaching and COVID came and retired the whole world for a time. Better get started on that memoir of mine, I said to no one but myself. I found I was making notes, sketching anecdotes of occasions where I had met writers, my contemporaries, and writers of the generation before me. I thought about calling the book *Name Dropping* but it wasn't dropping names exactly. To write, to read is a lonely business, produced and consumed, as it is, in private. COVID made that isolation more acute for me, for all of us. You wouldn't be surprised to know that the Statements of Purpose applicants send into the MFA programs all contain some variation of the wish to find a "community of writers." So, these dropped names are not dropped to impress, not the rubbing off of some notoriety or glossy celebrity, but a record of the tackiness (in the sense of "sticky" and not tactlessness) of how the paint dries on the infrastructure of accidents, introductions, acquaintances, friendships, and follies as well as the nostalgic ruins, tattered ephemera, and the sad sodden foxing at the edge of time and memory.

A book might seem to be constructed, manufactured, and published as if a writer writes something somewhere alone and then that written thing is sent away someplace and appears (pathogenetically!) a finished book to a reader out there somewhere. The middle of the middling is all camouflaged, disguised, the artifice of the artifice. But there, there in the mix of mixing, is a busy bumbling hive, of course, another community that is built to build a book, this book, while making it seem as if it just happened to happen.

So, who here to acknowledge then? First, there are the test kitchens of magazines and journals who published individual pieces. I thank the editors of *Big Other, The Texas Review, The Johns Hopkins Review,* and *The Offending Adam* for sampling early experiments in remembering. Most notably I must acknowledge Robert Stapleton, the editor of *Booth,* and his sous staff, graduate students at Butler University's MFA program, for not publishing a book per se of the complete smorgasbord of prose morsels but, much cooler, a special stand-alone section of *Booth 19* belly-banded to the magazine to boot. Cornerstone Press, commissary supreme, produced this final iteration of all my iterations and did so with all due speed, skill, and self-effacing stealth in difficult distracting times. I thank its director and publisher Ross K. Tangedal and the editing genius of Brett Hill and his staff, cover designer Scott Miller, as well as Ava Willett handling media and Sophie McPherson wrangling sales. Let me thank my agent who abides, Marian Young.

I could write right now a whole other book of Table Talk, acknowledging the younger generations writers I wrote with and who are still writing over the 40 years I taught at Iowa State, Harvard, and Syracuse Universities, Warren Wilson College, and the University of Alabama. The name dropping would be epic. But I am buoyed up by them, their murmuration, my murmuration, stretching from horizon to horizon.

I think I will begin that book, remembering all those tables, all those talks.

And there are the writers I wrote with and write to, breaking bread, colleagues name dropped here: Sandy Huss, Peter Streckfus, Kellie Wells, Dave Madden, Lex Williford, Joyelle McSweeney, Kate Bernheimer, Bruce Smith, Melanie Rae Thon, Hali Felt, Lamar Wilson, and Steve Pett.

More names, my first teachers: Dana Wichern, Robert Novak, John Flora, Margaret Wiggs, Kathleen Neuhaus, James Lewinski, Scott Sanders.

Susan Neville, Michael Wilkerson, Michael Rosen, Jonathan Strong, Dan Butler, Jay Brandon, Dinty W. Moore, and Jeremy Butler—all tattooed on my heart.

Obvious by now, my life is a pointillism of names, names tabbed, and memories dabbed at, all these stabs at getting the words right. Finishing the hat: Sam & Nick, Stella & Asa. And the first and final name: Theresa.

MICHAEL MARTONE is the author of over twenty books. He was born in Fort Wayne, Indiana, and now lives below the Bug Line in Tuscaloosa, Alabama. *Table Talk & Second Thoughts* is his second memoir, following *Michael Martone* (2005).

www.ingramcontent.com/pod-product-compliance
Lightning Source LLC
Chambersburg PA
CBHW020354130626
46549CB00006B/2285